Notes to Self:

A book of poetry and essays

of Jodi Schaap

on how she walked through the dark

until she found her light.

And she has so much to tell you.

Published in the United States by Ounce Publishing,
a division of An Ounce LLC, Michigan.

Names: Schaap, Jodi, author.

Title: Notes to self / Jodi Schaap

Description: Michigan: Ounce Publishing, 2024

Identifiers: ISBN 9798989906505 (paperback) /
9798989906512 (audio) / 9798989906529 (ebook)

Printed in the United States on acid-free paper.

jodimichelle.com

Book design by Jen Reimink

How to use this book:

Hello! I'm Jodi, the voice inside of these pages. Attracted to paper-look-books and typeface catalogs since I could read, I wanted Notes to Self to be a similar style of visual interest. This book is formatted to take you through my personal journey with every page standing alone as it's own poem.

Each chapter is marked by an intention for the following pages and walks through themes such as Loss, Pain. Grief, Anger, and so on, eventually reaching some acceptance and looking forward to the future.

When I started visualizing the book, I knew I wanted the cover to be bold and a little bit garish. The orange is a throwback to my high school binder where I wrote little poems and stuck stickers all over it, Notes to Self is a collection of poetry from the past 25 years of my life.

Visually, you'll see the formatting varies from poem to poem with graphics being introduced, first in black and white, then in color. None of this was a mistake. Not only will you see my poetry, you'll see my photographs, handwriting, and how I experience words.

Meant to be read cover to cover, this book is a love letter to myself. Quite literally notes to myself, the things I've picked up along the way, learned, tucked deep inside and want to keep forever. But you can use this book as a journal, to jot down your own conclusions and ideas. To keep track of your time, too. Or just to have for when you need a reminder that we're worth the work to love.

Let's get after it.

xoxo
Jodi

I will never regret letting the world watch me try
some of the most important people in it are my children,
and they have eyes.

1

I am going to write
like I'm running out of breath.

It will probably surprise no one that what I've been trying to do my entire life is remember who I am

And nothing reminds me more than the kitchen table. The stove, my grandmas hands, my grandpas fish. Ratty placemats and the devotional before prayer. How gathering with people who share my name feels like holy exercises in love.

I write poetry and essays, I have poetry eyes for life,

and I want to feed you.

I want to feed all of you with my heart.

This heart craves beets, not unlike the pounding of each and every beat in the bass drop. She wants vibrations, reverberations, iterations and cantations. To feel the earth beneath our feet as we pound all of this to the ground.

This heart that lives inside of me, she knows the difference between raw and well done.

———————

I want to be done performing for you,

bending in all the ways I don't fit inside of myself just to
be palatable for your preferences. Asking me to be your
surrogate scape goat of comfort isn't fair to either of us. To
any of us. I've gone rigid in my defiance to stand tall near
you, unmoving, unable to waver. And I want to be able to
dance again, to move my body and manage myself in a room
without worrying whether or not you approve.

So I'm done.
Right now, *this moment,* I declare myself capable.

You will feel neglect and shock and anger at my unwinding.
You will want to fix this.

But I am not for fixing.
I am for living.
I am for loving.

I am for leaving all of you behind.

———————

Am I afraid of ghosts? *(Laughs to self)*

Oh honey. They're my favorite companions.
Fables of another line, prophets of love, legends of time.

They tell the BEST stories.
They're our entire collection of fear,
packaged as lessons in love.

They tell you your favorite version
of the worst story over and over again
like kids around a campfire.
By the end of your disassociation:
you end up the hero of your own horror.

Showing you the way back to your own self.
She's here, she's there. She's everywhere.

You are the ghost.

———————

Sitting in the waiting room of my therapists office and there is clearly another session going on behind a closed door just to my left. An elderly woman is crying between questions from her therapist about her insurance coverage.

Her advice for the woman is generic at best.

I wonder if the woman feels heard, or just utterly defeated.

Would she feel supported knowing that everyone in the waiting room can hear her sorrow.

I wonder if anyone can hear me when I'm behind a different closed door, down the hall, quietly fighting each and every demon I keep comfortable in the darkest recesses of my body.

I wonder if I even care.

I check-in with myself, go inside and notice the sensations my body is sending up like sirens: it excites me a little, I'm tingling.

And I realize that what I care about most in this scenario is not who might be hearing me by accident, but who I need to hear me on purpose.

———————

I grew up all over the PNW. On the Badger and in my
memories of the Jackman Road farm, on the dirt road in
Texas and the creek behind Morningside drive. On Sleepy
Hollow, Pioneer, Perry, and 108th but mostly on Ardmore.
I grew up in the berry fields, in the trailer park off of Riley,
I split in two on Ransom, and I found God on Michelle Lane.
I grew up across the creek on Vanburen and down the street
from Kauw Park. I fell in love in the basement of my last
childhood home and I fell apart in my very first place, on my
own. I grew up in Chicago, down the aisles of every antique
store and in the maze of flea markets, along the I-90 and on
marathon road trips across the states. I grew up in Bangor,
Maine catching my dinner on the dock, kissing a boy under
the stars, braiding my hair and journaling for hours in a
motorhome. I grew up around my Aunt Ranae's kitchen table,
and flying standby all over the world and feeling like I could
run away and stay put and it would all actually be the same.

I grew up.

In Seattle, off of Berthusen, memorizing the Guide Meridian,
and River and where it turns to Butternut. On 35th St,
Vienna Strauss, and all over 8th street. In the kitchen of
Fairview Lane and all up and down Lakeshore drive, on M37,
I-96 and State street.

Where are you from, I hear people ask - and all I can think of
is *"right here."*

I will go broke loving well.

I want you to know that it
was never hard to love you

not even a little

not even kind of.

It's as if my body
is the mountainside,
laying down
for a while,
taking a rest
from this heavy work
of healing.

And out of my chest
a waterfall thunders through,
the moment
I name my feelings.

2

Here's the thing:
I'm no longer asking permission before I speak.

She had to die.

The former me, the scared little girl.

She lived a brave life, just not a full one.

And she had to die so I could finally live.

What have I been so afraid of?

If history repeats itself: I know where it ends up.

Right back here at the beginning.

But if I get to choose this time?

Well, then.

What am I waiting for?

———————

I'm no longer at war with those parts of me.
I've battled against her and I no longer can,
out of the best interest for my survival.
It is imperative you understand this is my decision.
Nothing you could have done, or didn't do,
would have persuaded me towards your idea of being me.
I have the experience needed to be the only voice
in that room from now on.

Thank you for your tireless tenure where,
without your persistent work ethic and ability
to find shame in the smallest most meaningless places:
I wouldn't have been pushed far enough
beyond my conditioning to see the rug
being pulled from right beneath me.

———————

No one else is on this journey, with me.
I am in the wilderness of my own undoing - and it's
breathtaking, sacred, and horrifying.
I am fighting my way towards safety
through all the thorns and thickets of your warfare.
I identify landmines in my sleep, careful to disarm them
before I wake, not to worry my bedfellow or family.
I am ok.
I am ok.
I am ok.
I will be ok.
I think I will be ok, will I be ok?

North is where the moss grows on trees and where I live -
West is where the water lives. And somewhere deep inside of
me is where I keep the key.

Where nothing about me resembles the life you had planned
for the end of We.

———————

David didn't beat Goliath by assuming his defeat because the probability of his success was low.

He got in the ring, with the only tool he had available to him.

So don't come at me about your projected fears because #scary.

I stand in the dark all the time, and it's because I'm visible that other people can see.

Some people talk with their hands,
littering the air with their punctuation fists and elbows.
But I talk with my whole face,
seeing for the first time or reliving this exact moment again;
the only way you'll understand what I mean is when you pay
attention to where my eyes dart.

Em-dashes of my mind.
Every breath a comma,
every intentional pause a period.
My hands might creep up as an aide
but what I'm really saying - all of the time - is are you even
paying attention?

———————

3

I will be trapped here for as long as I am here,
you understand that right?

BECAUSE it is *Difficult*

NOT

to be an

ANGRY

Woman

these

DAYS

Be small,

stay silent,

calm down,

you're too excited.

I just don't know how not to.

My entire life has been a very careful prescription of shining just enough to pass the test but never more.

I have been controlling the illumination, tightly winding myself up its coil to stop it from being seen

Because I was never told, but always taught, that to shine brighter than you would

Be the death of me.

―――――――――

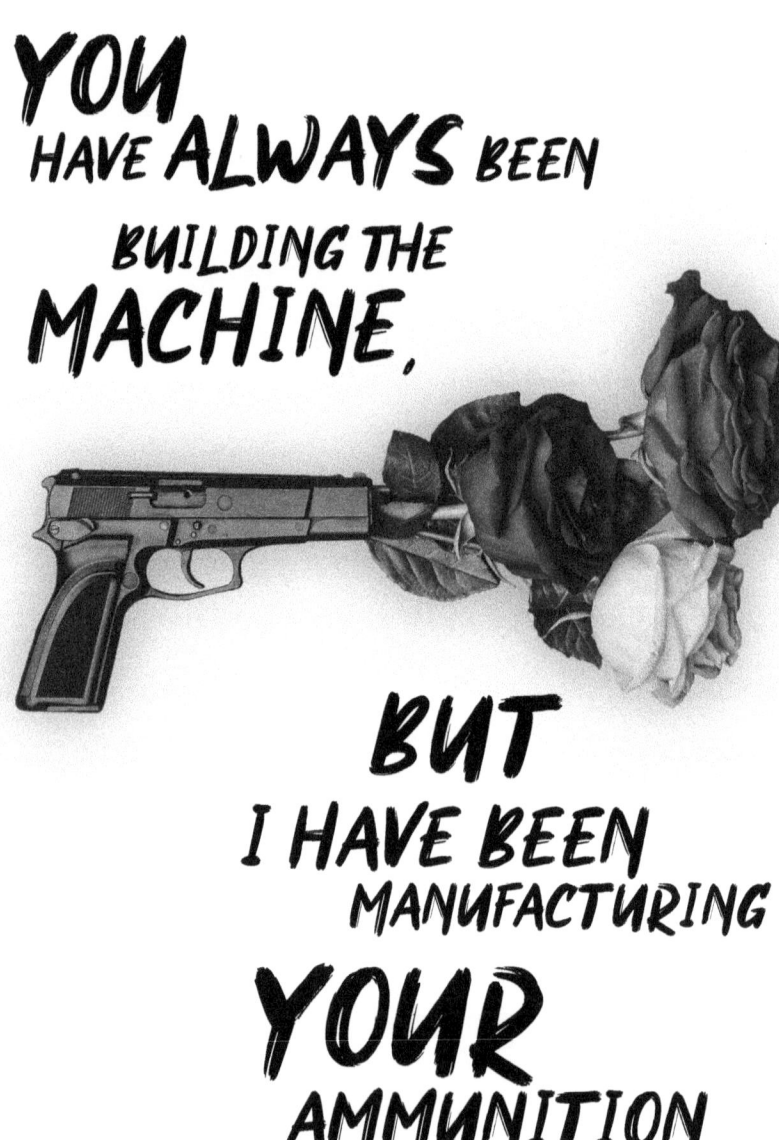

YOU HAVE **ALWAYS** BEEN BUILDING THE **MACHINE,**

BUT I HAVE BEEN MANUFACTURING **YOUR** AMMUNITION

People take my silence
as permission to continue their behavior.

Gossip?

Give me unsolicited advice?

Correct my concerns with your conspiracy?

Push me, pull me, puppet me for pleasure?

It's funny you haven't figured this out yet,
but you're on borrowed time.

An unsuccessful game of tug of war is happening,
you have a rope around my neck and any moment now

Yes,

I'll test the resilience of your anger when I stop letting you
shove me off this cliff.

Rigid, I become, in the wake of your defiance.
Unwilling to move an inch until you see your own reflection.

———————

I'm tired of being the Virgin Mary for every man who wants an excuse to tell me what I was made for.

I wasn't made for you.

Adam was one and done. Have you even read the creation story? Every woman is not your Eve. Not your helper, not your shelter.

You want to spread your seed?

Invest in socks. I will not fortify this bond.

———————

Obedience isn't the dirty
word you think of

My breasts aren't knobs
for you to press

This conversation is so
one sided

Why can't you contain
your own mess?

YOU WANT TO CONTROL ME? STRAP IN. OBJECTS OF MY DESTRUCTION ARE CLOSER THAN THEY APPEAR.

I have been provoked enough.

Trained to be silent, but ready. To be quiet, but pretty.
To be good, but small. To be safe, but never fall.

You're always watching me.

Sit down.

I know why the caged bird sings ... because her song is a siren

for

me.

———

what you think i should do

You know what has never ever been up for debate as it relates to my body? What you think I should do. This is a new practice for me, because as a child I was not given agency over my self. I didn't know I was allowed to advocate for my person: I never learned how.. Sure, I was told a few times as a teenager that no means no. But that would-be-power came too late.

What about all the time before that? All the instances where I wanted someone to ask me, or respect me: had I been able to say no then? They were ignored, any way. Who did I think I was? My own.

4

I'm always racing against something,

My time,

My mind,

A task,

This mask.

I have been your portal for pain, never letting it land on me, even when it was meant to. I have worked tirelessly to avoid your shrapnel.

But what I didn't discover, until now, was that with every battle; I wouldn't let you see me wince while I buried your words, actions, and absence deep inside.

An expert at this vanishing act, I've ignored the throbbing for ages. But I can't any more.

What you wanted to shape me, shifted. I am not the girl you got to dream up: I am who all of this made me.

When you've systematically worked
at erasing someone from your life,
is it when they've disappeared
that you know you're done?

Or when you ask for them
and they never come.

———————

I used
to think that
I needed pain
to be honest

But what I
really needed
was to be honest
about my pain

When your daughter asks for more after
you have already given everything you have for her:
Do you tell her the truth

Or Lie a little more

If I could exhale into my full skin,
I would take up the entire room.

I would fill it with so much love,
so much comfort and joy.

I would lower my shoulders, finally,
laugh loudly and sit straight up.

Learning that by letting things go,
I can grow taller, yes.

But also kinder.

I can grow more tolerant and patient.

When I stop holding my entire universe
together with the tension I can create in my
stomach - achingly on guard for all of this
bullshit.

———————

Did you know that in all the aftermath of our yesterdays we can visit ourselves and start anew.

Did you know healing felt so raw, like road rash near the pickle factory. Each (re)discovery another throbbing itch you can't find.

Did you know how much safety would cost? Did you even inquire.

Did you know that lying to me would be this pervasive, that I would never forget, that I would build my trust on the back of your heels turned to the sky from your begging stance for me to see it your way.

Did you know?

Did you even know I have always known this about you?

Did you know you taught me everything about nothing at all.

———————

true or false: you loved me
true or false: you wanted me
true or false: you left me
true or false: you love me

You know the kind of
pain that hurts?

Mine is the kind that
will make it burst

Will we measure your impact by the ripples you left behind, generations of whispers and stories circulating the world like the magic that you are?

Or by the crater with which you left us in.

———————

I've led him to believe

that my biggest insecurity

was my body

when all along

it has been if I've ever

been enough.

Jodi,
listen to the
truth you know
deep inside.

let it be
true. let it
be true.

And then
let it
be.

XO

On therapy

I just witnessed myself surviving ... for years.

Each and every instance of complete terror, paralyzing confusion, abrupt loneliness.

Every trespass on my mind, body and soul.

And this time, I told myself the truth

Then let the rest go.

———————

5

How many times have I tried to start over?

Why don't I, instead, just try to keep going?

I have tried to be who I thought you saw me as,
without asking for instructions,
I just decided I understood the assignment
and didn't look back.

I have so many questions, now.
So many notes and ideas.
Maybe I could just be me, after all.

———————

Let it be known that my tolerance for pain has always been sky high. It's not that I never felt it, it's that I was never taught what it was I was feeling.

And now I feel it in my bones, in the aches and muscle spasms. In the absence of a loving touch, instead of an embrace.

Where my ligaments and the sinew tissue of my flesh now scream for relief, I can recognize her nerves ending. I can trace the scars back to the battles and the tears back to the blood.

And my tolerance hasn't grown weaker, but my threshold grew wiser.

I don't need your explanation anymore; I learned to first ask myself what happened instead.

———————

Do you find solace and comfort in this war you have waged against me? Tirelessly workshopping your angles to benefit your narrative where getting caught only fuels your shooting-spree?

You enjoy this? The tension you've sewn where peace should be? Each and every word colored a different shade of grey only you can see?

Have you ever wanted to tell someone to fuck all the way off?

Because I just did.

And it set me free.

———————

I HAVE A LOT OF FEELINGS BECAUSE I'M ALLOWED TO FEEL THINGS

I will not be careful anymore I am not fragile in the
Way
You believe
I have the capacity

To

Be

In those ways, I am stronger than you'll ever know.
Patient, willing, slow.

But in the fury, in the everlasting power struggle for my mind:

I am unstoppable.

———————

I've carried your sadness for so long that I didn't have room for any of mine.

So I put yours down

and let mine wash over me

like a wave, like a blanket, like a baptism

Brand new.

———————

I need to stop braiding my future
with the roots of my past.

———

6

Shame is not a megaphone,
it's a muffler.

I will ▮ not ▮
▮ water ▮
▮ down the ▮
realities ▮ of ▮
▮ life ▮
▮ and ▮ replace
▮ them ▮
with ▮ the ▮
▮ principles of
▮ your ▮ faith.

I am
the girl
of my
dreams

I no longer visit the gravesites

of the lives I never lived

———————

I'm not ashamed of it.
I'm aware of it.

One matters.

I made these people my purpose,

but what happens

when they find their own

———————

Outside council shouldn't have the voting rights on your own decisions.

You have to choose.

Something must have happened to my
elemental makeup to no longer want to
mother every baby I see.

I don't crave the weight of someone else's
potential on my hip, any longer.

Or maybe; I discovered my own and it's no
longer tethered to other.

———————

I'm just not gonna do it
your way anymore.

I'm gonna do it
my way.

It's funner.

I just decided not to anymore.

Not to keep track
Not to hold back

———

7

I've known all along. I protected her the way I so
badly wanted someone, anyone, to protect me.

I don't know how to turn the truth down.

It's loud,
like a ringing church bell in my heart,

swaying

swaying

swaying

heavy in a metal gown

She bellows, it rings, I sway
She hollers, it sings, I obey

I USED TO WANT
THE WORST
FOR YOU
BUT I DISGUISED
IT AS WHAT WAS
BEST FOR ME

I'M SUSPECT OF
PEOPLE WHO ARE
SURPRISED BY
HONESTY

Empire

If my body was a moat

where would the river flow?

I have never built anything just for me.

It's always been for all of us.

Because I know deep down that we are worth the effort to see
it through. See this magnificent life to its fullest moments.
To shout I love you's and color outside the lines. We're worth
the work to love. To be celebrated and given our wildest
dreams.

Just because.

I have never built anything just for me.

It's always been for us.

———————

TEACHING MY CHILDREN HOW TO

ASK
FOR
HELP

IS THE MOST HELPLESS THING I DO.

Why does it sound like explaining a map to my son when giving him all I have to offer.

Directions, memories, responses.

Memorization of facts and dates and places and remember this house: this is the safe house.

And please, please don't forget this road sign, it points to the place where we always find each other again.

And wait!

What about these coordinates: keep these somewhere safe - they're the key to my heart, forever yours.

And why does it sound like singing a love song over my daughter when giving her all I have to offer.

The real ones, true ones and one hit wonders.

Memorization of facts and dates and places and remember this house: this is the safe house.

And please, please don't forget where you find joy, it points to the place where you always find yourself.

And wait!

What about these moments - keep them tucked away;

they're your inner strength, the absolute beauty of who you are: once a part of me, always a piece of me: forever yours.

————————

YOU EVER THINK ABOUT
MEETING NEW PEOPLE LATER
IN LIFE AND WONDER HOW
MUCH THEY'LL JUST NEVER KNOW
ABOUT YOU BECAUSE OF WHEN THEY
CAME INTO YOUR LIFE AND DOES IT
EVER MAKE YOU SAD THAT YOUR
LIVED EXPERIENCE HAS AN
EXPIRATION DATE AND ALMOST
NO ONE CHECKS IT.

8

This is what I've learned:
if I'm at the edge of my own capacity ...
whatever comes next will take my breath away.

THOSE GIRLS

I'm living like
I'm dying.
Take notes.

You do not have to perform
to be loved

You do not have to perform
to be loved

You do not have to perform

to be

loved

COWARDS NEVER RISE

If you can't tell me in
one sentence
why your life fell apart,

It didn't.

You just changed your mind
And that's enough.

You won't be effective

in ministry

if you're

constantly offended

by the people

you're supposed to

be loving.

———————

LOVE DOESN'T NEED A DEFENSE BUT FEAR ALWAYS DOES.

We all deserve
our own kind
of justice

It's not justice
if it isn't also
for us

Stop running away from everything you already have.

Let this be enough.

Where does your
shadow sleep?

Broken hearts
are allowed
to heal
in the middle
of all of
your mundane.

You're allowed to
let what people say
BE what people have said.

You can believe what they are
trying to tell you.

———

It's ok not to have
something to give
sometimes.

That's why the word
receive exists.

I THINK

THE MOST IMPORTANT

THING TO REMEMBER

WHEN LEARNING

WHO YOU ARE

IS NOT TO WEAR

WHAT OTHER

PEOPLE THINK

Literally cannot with your extremism.

Unless you're extremely happy,
and it's contagious.

Unless you're gifted and willing to share.

Unless you're quiet in a room full of loud talkers.

Unless you're willing to go first, no longer
requiring me to do the work for you.

Unless you are extremely compassionate, like
a champion for the broken in a room full of
samesame.

We are not endangered, we are IN danger.
There is a difference.

It is our hearts.

———

Watch me carry you.

You are not
too heavy for me.

I'll be specific.
If I die before you:
celebrate the shit out of my life.

Read poetry and love letters,
even if they're not from me.
Tell everyone they're amazing.
Sing songs. Dance. Dance louder.
Eat food, the messy kind.
Let it drip like the tears on your cheeks,
get drunk and dance some more.

Love wildly.

With absolute abandon.

Go apeshit for each other and

Tell

Everyone

The

Truth.

———————

Let's get to the place where we don't feel bad anymore.
Let's numb the moral upbringing we can't seem to shake,
let's find each other in the storm of our yesterdays,
let's give the other a pass for the bullshit we didn't know
how to deal with when we could have been learning how
to deal with each other.

Let's let this go: let's turn it up and on and let's move
towards one another.

Show me where I was missed.

Tell me where I'm going to be kissed.

I want this.

———————

9

Guilt was my first teacher.
But, Hope will be my last.

I used to think about other people, strangers really, as if they had the exact same life as me. Behind closed doors they were being loved and they were loving their children. Behind closed doors they were making lists, doing laundry, timing themselves at bath-time duty and anticipating quiet. Behind closed doors they were naive and held innocent beliefs about grief and love and loss. I would pass cars on the road and think, they must be going to the store, too. Running errands, ticking off responsibilities, like me. We were all floating; tethered by my experiences. I was driving my honda civic with my toddler in the backseat, listening to music, when a similar car passed me from oncoming traffic and I realized: we're all living our own lives. A sliding door moment I can never forget and suddenly everyone was interesting. I would look people in the eyes at the grocery store or at stop signs, while waiting for a train and I would ask them in my mind if they were looking for their answers, too. Some of them seemed to understand my question with their softening looks and small smiles. Were they seeing me, then, like I was seeing them? Wholly apart from who I was and also the only thing that mattered? When they looked away I would evaluate the information I had taken in. If they looked down and to the left to avoid my inquiry, they knew something but couldn't share it with me. If they darted away at the sight of my wonder, they were practicing invisibility and wanted to be left alone. If they peered back at me, unwavering, I knew we understood each other. Right there in the middle of our mundane: being seen. And I started asking different questions: are you happy here? are you safe? do you know how loved you are? has anyone ever cried over you, like I'm about to? has anyone ever believed in your dreams or taught you how? did someone wake up loving you today and you just don't know it yet? are we all going to be ok?

Well it turns out coming home to yourself is slow motion,
not a singular happenstance.

It happens in every moment we tell ourselves the truth,
in every moment we honor her whispers.

It happens like a long walk around a lake.

Slowly at first, and then with purpose.

What if?

you accept this love?

you learn to love bigger?

you take chances?

———

Today, I'm a lung.

In whatever universe that matters —
today I can inhale deeply.

Arms wide open,
I am taking everything in.

I am a lung.

You can run.

I believe there is a God

When I read a book by an amateur cook turned author on how to boil water and it inspires me to want to buy anchovies, have chickens, shop from my local farmer with purpose (not passive activism) because there's something inside of me that knows this is true.

I believe there is a God

When people whom I look up to dare to say the unlucky statements and break tradition with religious stigma to be the branch for all Gods people. Not just the ones 'we' prefer.

I believe there is a God

When the simple act of helping my loved ones lights a fire I cannot contain. My core shakes with vulnerability because I let my light shine and they saw it ... and called me "good".

I believe there is a God

When we identify our darkness instead of pretending we can't color in those shades. When we see the bleak across the way and recognize our own life in those ashes. It's no longer "I could never" as much as it is "I can see how" and in that statement, that posture - we hold open our arms to the resurrecting grace of the gospel. There is darkness in every one of us. "Me, too" isn't just a movement, it's the tiniest act of kindness you'll ever have to utter to form a bridge. Which is all kinds of resistance, all kinds of scandal for our dark and lonely sufferings.

I believe there is a God

When I'm 50,000 feet above the ground soaring through the clouds on a metal boat in the air and it seems like we're the only ones in the entire world in the middle of the sky. To see the sand I feel beneath my toes from this perspective, unrecognizable. To know how many people and lives and hearts and souls are aimlessly, or gloriously, walking around and driving and going to school or playing outside or making love - I just can't help but think: so this is what you see ... Everything. All of us, all of it. You see the whole picture. And for a moment, just a moment, I'm filled with peace.

(An everlasting meal, by Tamar Adler - I've read just the first chapter. It's titled "How to Boil Water" and she brought God alive for me in those pages. Chapter two, which I'm about to dig into, is titled "How to Teach an Egg to Fly" and I have to be honest: there's no telling what comes next for me.

I have decided not to hate you

but instead learn to love you with all your imperfections.

I have decided to accept you, in all your width and wrinkles.

I have decided not to hate how soft we are together

how easy you are to please

how happy you are in laughter

how jubilant you become while dancing

how moved we feel in your sadness

how careful I am not to hurt you

how hard it is when I do, anyway.

I have decided not to hate you anymore.

But to love you for being with me

in every bad situation, in every scary conversation,

in every triggering moment,

in every piece of ecstasy, in all our loneliness,

in the moments that broke me open, wide

and without permission, in every untimely birth,

and every single breath thereafter.

I have decided to love all of you

especially the parts I've worked so hard to forget

You have a place here, too. With us.

Together.

I have decided not to hate you, after all.

Because I love all of you, any way.

———————

Hi there. I'm so glad you've reached the end of this book. For as long as I can remember, I've been a writer.

And it delights me to no end that now you hold in your hands the very thing I have always known was supposed to exist. Thank you for your support, if we're just meeting for the first time through these words; my name is Jodi and I believe the best in people.

I'm lucky to have some of the best people to thank for helping me get here today, like my friend, Jen, she works at the print shop in a small town who prints my work, she designed the layout and went through years and years of trial and error prints with me. And Brian, for letting her skip work whenever we have a great idea to run away. (How's Thursday, Jen??!!)

To my mom for the unwavering support, even when it hurt her to hear my honesty, she is a steadfast body of peace and connection for me. Thank you to my friends who have quietly (yet confidently) kept after me to see this through. The small nudges, encouraging words, the simple act of being interested: this is for all of us.

Now to my family who have been along for the whole ride, patient with my process, and accepting of all the faults I continue to confess to them. They know I prefer physical comedy to almost anything else; they love to surprise me, but hate how it makes me cry and they know if it were up to me - Hugs would be a valid currency.

Aaron, Jessica and Oliver: ya basic ...ally the best. I love us. Thank you.

xoxo mom

www.ingramcontent.com/pod-product-compliance
Lightning Source LLC
Chambersburg PA
CBHW051326120626
46547CB00015B/2409